D1314492

Drawing in Space

Hello and welcome to *Drawing in Space*. What is space?

If you travel beyond our planet, Earth, you will eventually reach outer space. Our universe contains many objects, such as planets, moons, stars, solar systems, and galaxies. A solar system is a group of planets revolving around a star. Our solar system is centered around the sun, which is a huge star, and it is part of a larger galaxy called the Milky Way. In between all these different objects are huge, empty gaps known as space.

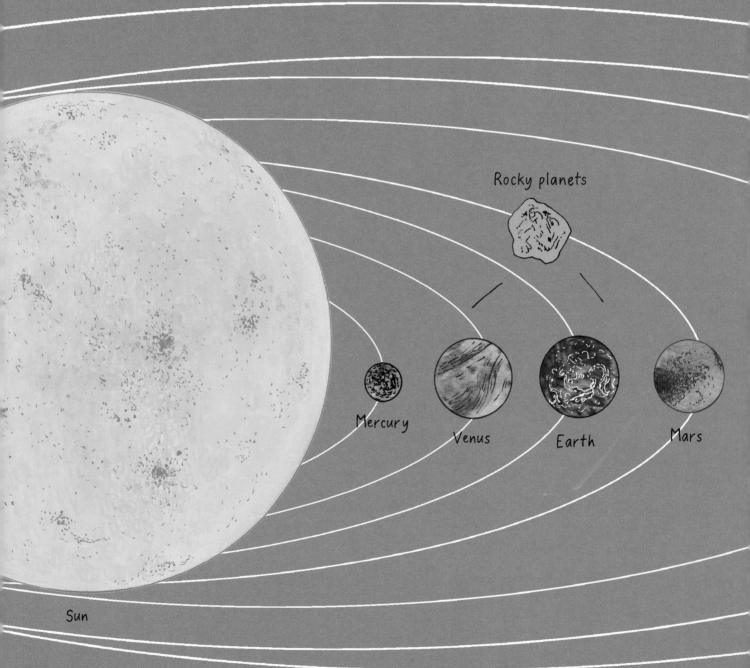

Rocky planets

Mercury

Venus

Earth

Mars

Sun

Rock and Gas
There are eight planets altogether:
four are rocky and four are gaseous.

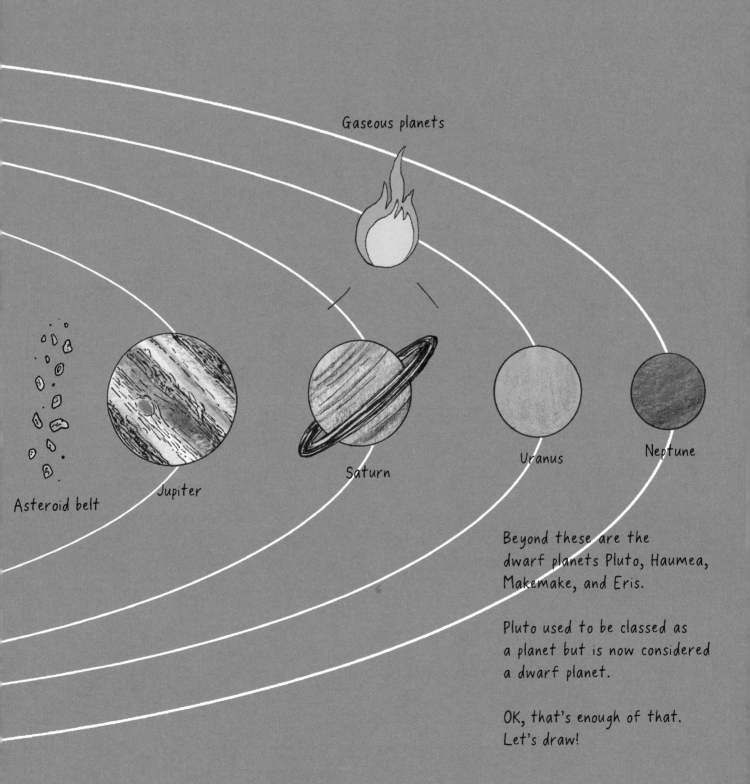

Gaseous planets

Asteroid belt

Jupiter

Saturn

Uranus

Neptune

Beyond these are the
dwarf planets Pluto, Haumea,
Makemake, and Eris.

Pluto used to be classed as
a planet but is now considered
a dwarf planet.

OK, that's enough of that.
Let's draw!

THe BIG BANG!

How did space begin? Some scientists think the universe started with a huge explosion that happened billions of years ago. It is known as the big bang. The material from the explosion gradually spread and cooled, eventually forming all the galaxies, stars, planets, and moons in the universe. It is still expanding today!

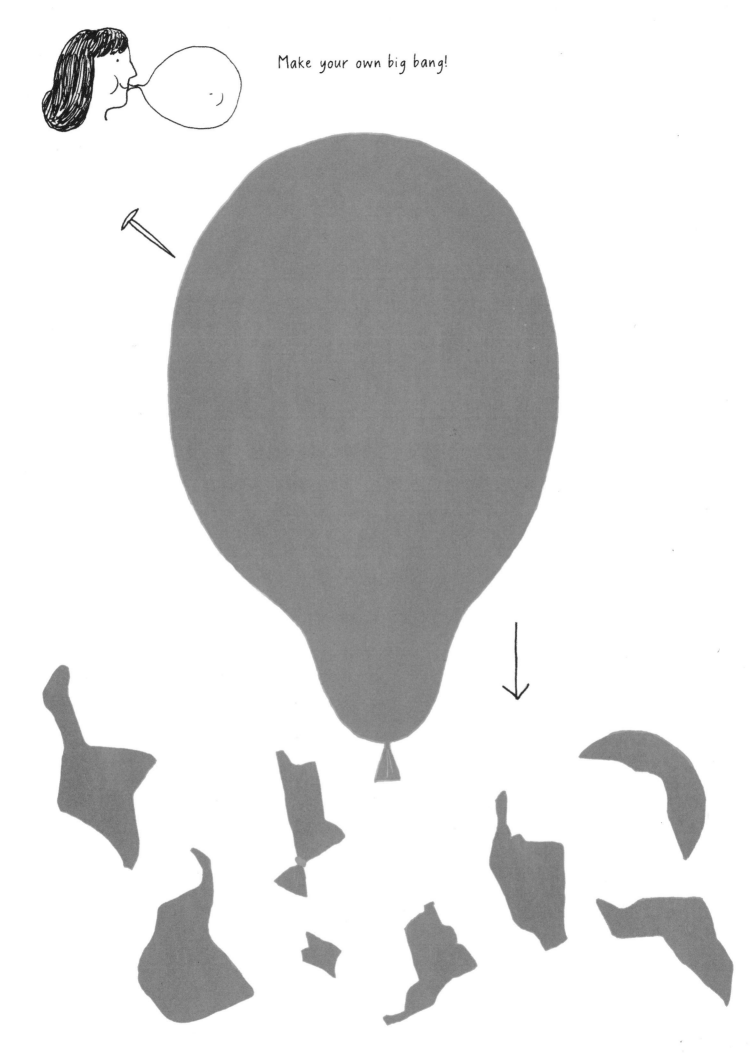

Make your own big bang!

Where does space begin?

Earth is wrapped in a huge blanket of gases called the atmosphere. The atmosphere has five layers: the troposphere, the stratosphere, the mesosphere, the thermosphere, and the exosphere.

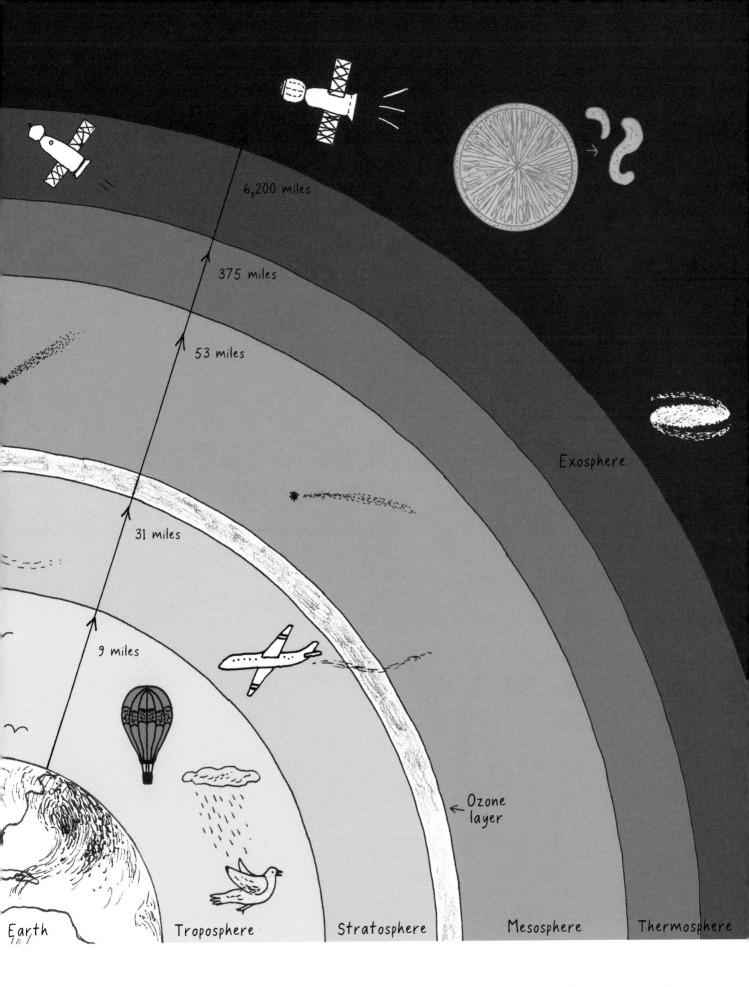

6,200 miles

375 miles

53 miles

31 miles

9 miles

Exosphere

Ozone layer

Earth

Troposphere

Stratosphere

Mesosphere

Thermosphere

If the Earth were an orange, the atmosphere would only be as thick as the skin of the orange!

The outer part of the atmosphere is where space begins, about 6,200 miles from Earth!

The sun

The sun is actually a star, the closest one to Earth, found at the center of our solar system. It is extremely important, providing light, warmth, and energy necessary for life on our planet.

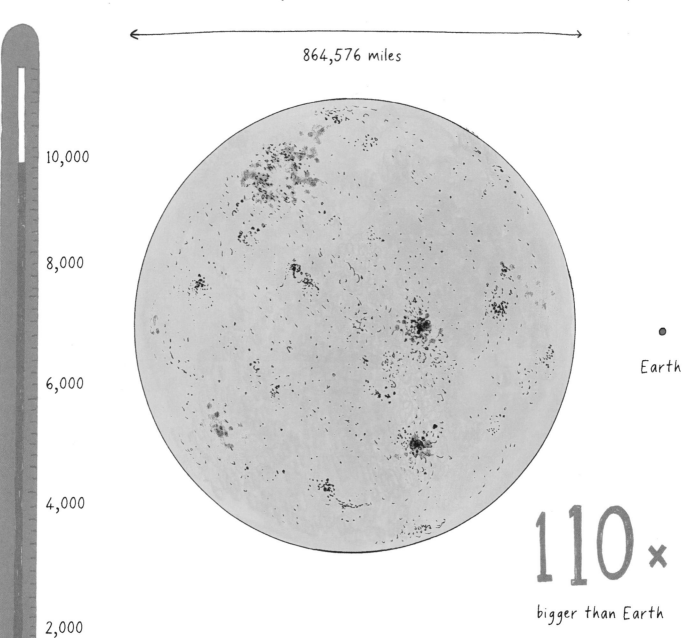

864,576 miles

10,000

8,000

6,000

4,000

2,000

Earth

110 ×

bigger than Earth

The sun is hotter than the hottest thing you can imagine. It is a huge ball of burning gases with a surface temperature of 9,941 degrees Fahrenheit. Its core is even hotter!

Even though the sun is so far away from us, it can be dangerous to be out in the sun for too long, especially if you have fair skin.

On very sunny days, it is a good idea to wear sunglasses. Draw some sunglasses to protect these eyes from the hot sun!

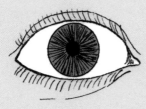 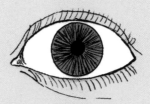

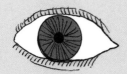 

the MOON

Earth has one moon. It orbits Earth in twenty-nine and a half days.

What does the moon look like?

The moon lights up our night sky. It seems to change shape—sometimes it looks like a perfect, round, glowing globe and at other times like a thin crescent. And sometimes we can't see it at all!

The dark side of the moon

The moon is covered in craters, which are round hollows. It's a bit like a golf ball!

The moon reflects light, just like a disco ball!

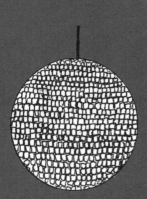

Some people can see a face in the moon.

Can cows jump over the moon?

Some people think the moon is made of green cheese.

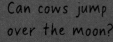

Phases of the moon

Earth

Full moon

Moon

Day   Night

The moon does not emit its own light; instead, it reflects light from the sun. The moon's position in relation to the sun means that its shape appears to keep changing, depending on how much of the sunlit side we can see.

Alternative phases of the moon

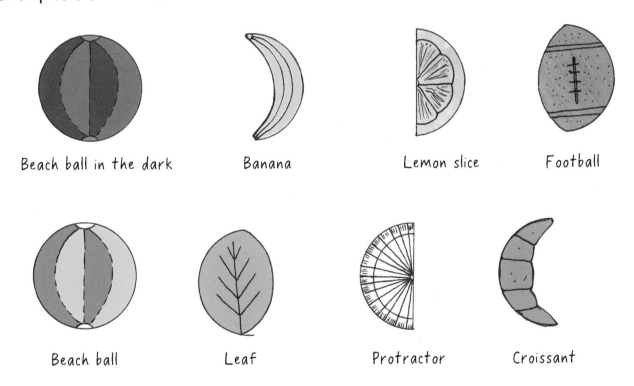

Beach ball in the dark

Banana

Lemon slice

Football

Beach ball

Leaf

Protractor

Croissant

Draw your own version of the moon.

EARTH

Earth is the only planet with known life. Most of its surface is covered in water, and oxygen is plentiful. Both water and oxygen are essential for living things.

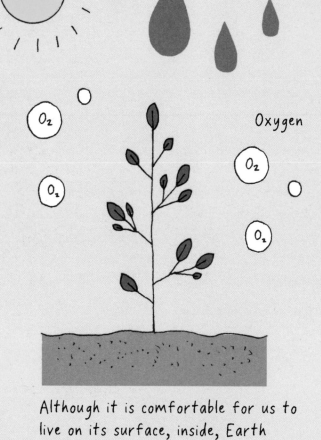

Oxygen

O₂ O₂ O₂ O₂

GRAVITY

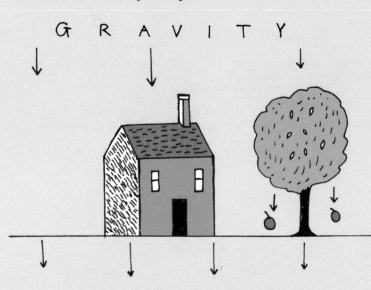

The Earth is moving all the time, although we cannot feel it. Everything on Earth is held down by a force called gravity. If there were no gravity, everything would float away!

Although it is comfortable for us to live on its surface, inside, Earth has an extremely hot core.

Apple core

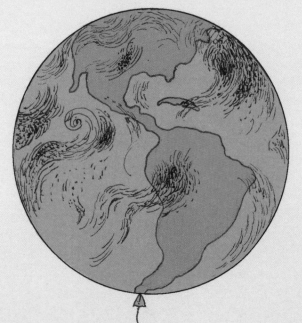

Gravity also keeps Earth in its place on its journey around the sun. Without gravity, Earth would float away like a huge balloon.

Imagine if there were no gravity.
Draw some things floating away!

Mercury →

Mercury is the planet closest to the sun, so it is very hot. It is the smallest planet and also the fastest, taking only eighty-eight days to orbit around the sun.

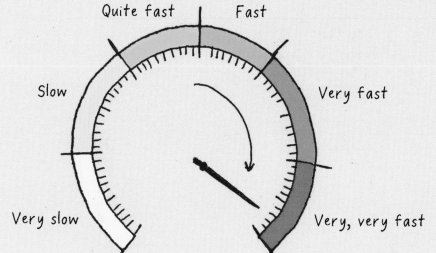

Quite fast   Fast

Slow   Very fast

Very slow   Very, very fast

There is mercury in this thermometer, too, but a different type of mercury!

Draw some other fast-moving things.

The peregrine falcon is the fastest bird.

The cheetah is the fastest animal.

Mercury is the fastest planet.

Venus

Venus is sometimes called Earth's sister. It is very similar in size and made up of the same rocks and metals as Earth. It has volcanoes, mountains, and sand, but no water. It would be impossible for humans to live there as the air is toxic and the surface as hot as a furnace!

Earth

What do you think the sisters are saying to each other? Do they get along?

Draw some life on Earth.

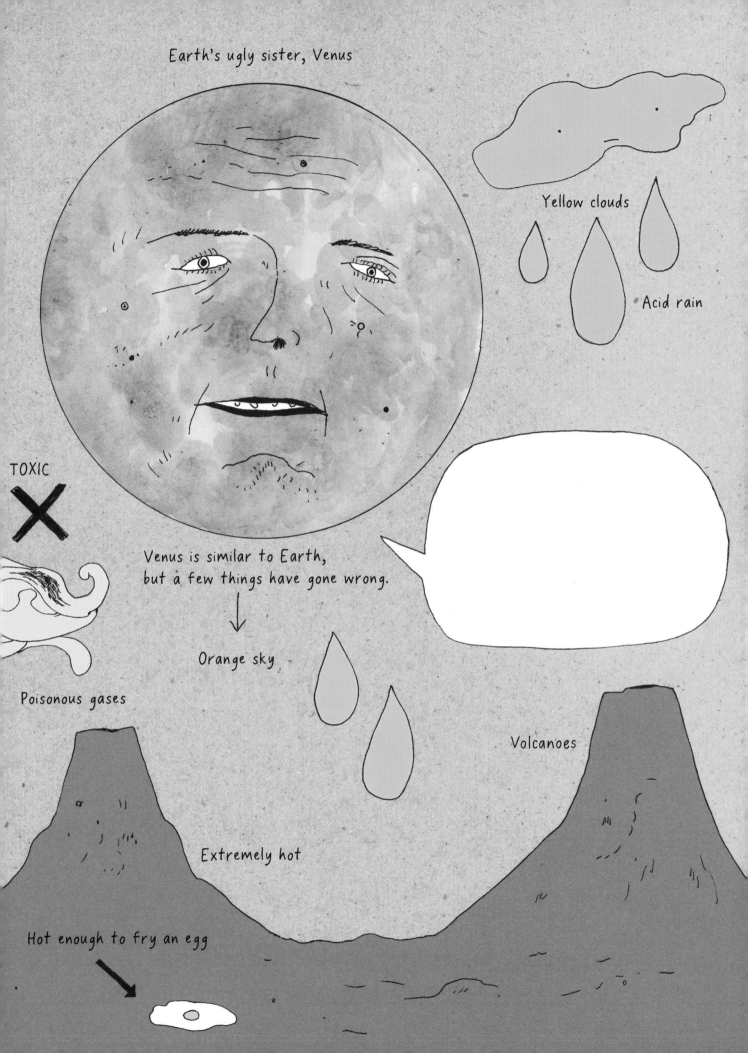

MARS

– – – – – –

Mars is sometimes called the red planet because its surface is a huge, red, dusty desert.

It was once believed that there were canals on Mars, built by an alien civilization.

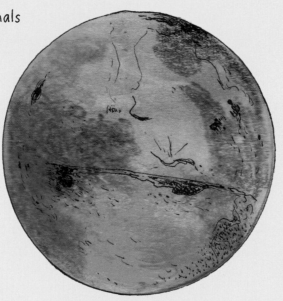

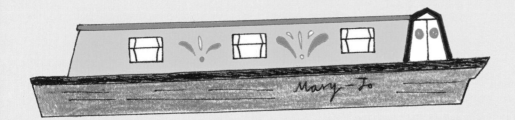

Mary Jo

Draw some canal boats on Mars.
Who is traveling on them?

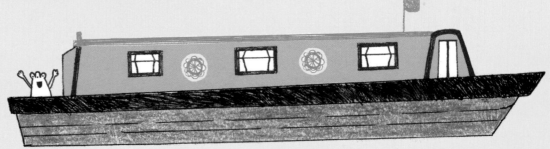

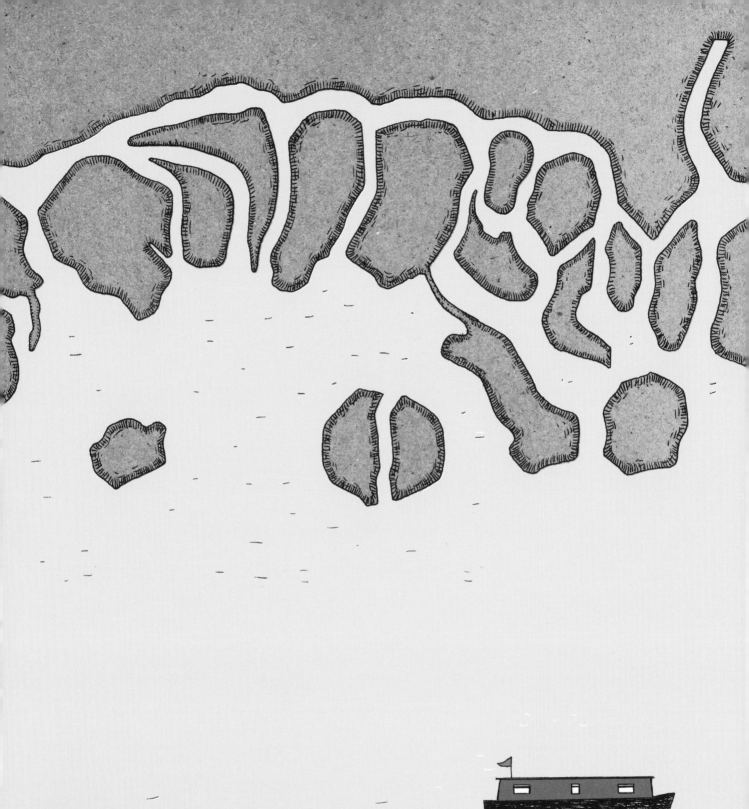

Asteroid Belt

Between Mars and Jupiter is a huge ring of space rocks known as the asteroid belt. Asteroids are rocks left over from when the planets and their satellites were formed.

Draw some asteroids into the belt.

Smaller pieces of rock are known as meteoroids.

They are called meteors once they pass into Earth's atmosphere!

Most asteroids look like small boulders, but some are much bigger. Ceres is the size of France! It is such a huge asteroid that it is called a dwarf planet.

Jupiter

Jupiter is the largest planet in the solar system.
It has alternating dark and light stripes. Sometimes a large red spot is visible.

Jupiter's red spot is actually an enormous, raging storm.

Jupiter has more than sixty moons. Here are two of them. Can you draw the rest? Use your imagination!

Jupiter's red spot is three times wider than Earth!

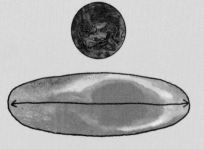

This poor boy also has a large red spot.
His name is Danny.

Danny's spot is a nasty
pimple on his skin. It
can be treated with
spot cream.

Danny doesn't have
any moons, but
perhaps he would like
some. Or maybe he
would prefer sweets?
Draw some.

Saturn

Saturn is a large planet surrounded by many colored rings.
Here are some other kinds of rings:

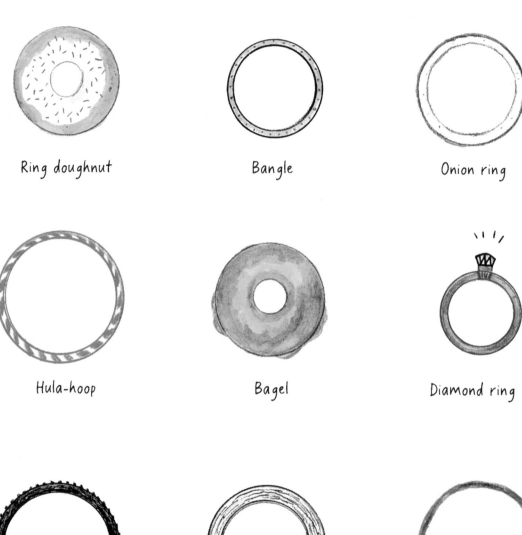

Ring doughnut

Bangle

Onion ring

Hula-hoop

Bagel

Diamond ring

Bicycle tire

Roll of sticky tape

Rubber band

Saturn's rings are actually nothing like any of these—they are made up of icy rocks of many different shapes and sizes. The icy chunks are like mirrors that reflect the light of the sun, making the rings appear to glow.

What other kinds of rings can you think of? Draw some rings around Saturn.

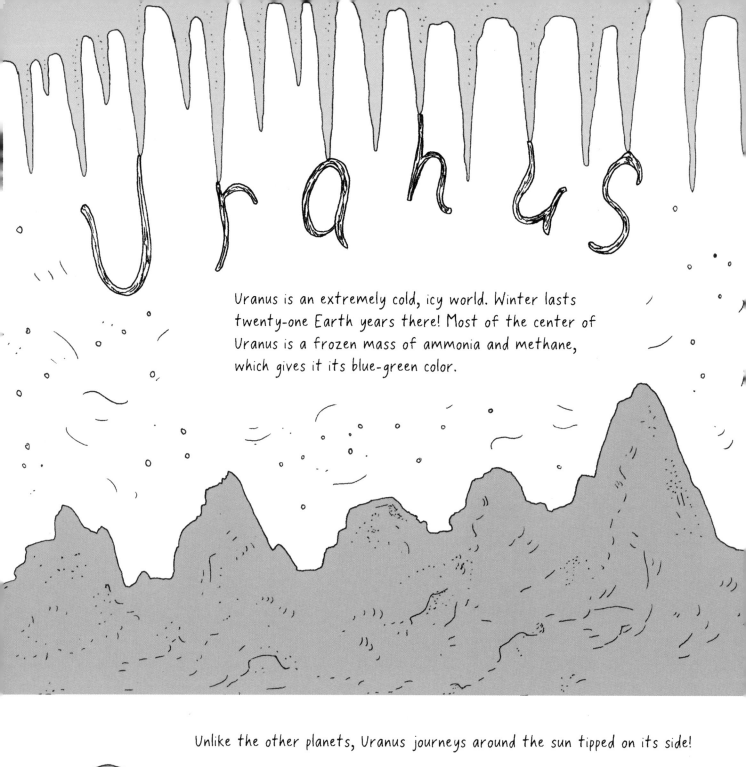

Uranus

Uranus is an extremely cold, icy world. Winter lasts twenty-one Earth years there! Most of the center of Uranus is a frozen mass of ammonia and methane, which gives it its blue-green color.

Unlike the other planets, Uranus journeys around the sun tipped on its side!

Imagine a sideways world.

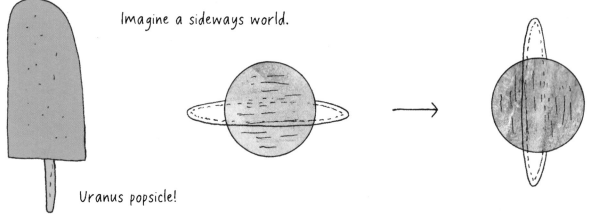

Uranus popsicle!

Draw some sideways skaters and winter-sports fans on Uranus!

Neptune

1,300 mph

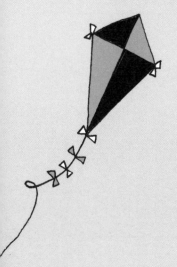

Neptune is the eighth and furthest planet from the sun. It is also the windiest planet. Winds on Neptune can reach up to 1,300 miles per hour. That's ten times faster than a hurricane!

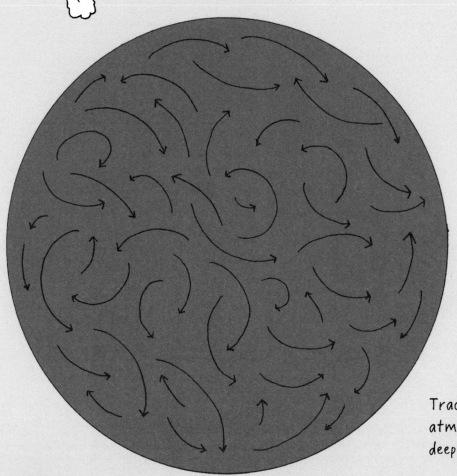

Traces of methane in Neptune's atmosphere give the planet a deep blue color.

Draw some windmills on Neptune!

Wind turbine

Wind sock

Pinwheel

Pluto and the dwarf planets

Hi, I'm Pluto...

...and I'm not happy.

Do you want to know why?

For years and years I was considered a planet.

I had eight lovely planet friends. We used to have such fun traveling around the sun.

But in 2006, that all changed. My planet status got taken away!

I got reclassified. The memory still pains me...

Do you know what they started calling me?

A dwarf planet!

I mean, can you imagine how I felt? What had I done to deserve this? Nothing, I tell you!

A dwarf planet...

I'm an outcast...

Oh, hello! I'm Eris. Who are you?

I'm Pluto. Are you a planet?

No, I'm a dwarf planet.

Oh, really? I didn't realize there were other dwarf planets like me!

Yes, there are lots of us. Meet Haumea and Makemake, too!

Oh, hello! We think there may be even more of us out there.

Really? Yes, do you want to help us look?

Oh, yes. I feel much happier now.

Come on, then!

There are five known dwarf planets:

Eris   Pluto   Haumea   Makemake   Ceres

Astronomers believe there may be many more dwarf planets in existence.
Draw some more dwarf planets. Can you name them, too?

The Odd One Out

Apart from being the only planet able to support life, Earth is the odd one out for another reason. All the other planets besides Earth are named after ancient gods in Roman mythology.

Mercury, god of speed

Venus, goddess of love and beauty

Earth

Mars, god of war

Match the god to the planet.

Jupiter, king of the gods

Saturn, god of agriculture

Uranus, god of the sky

Neptune, god of the sea

Universe

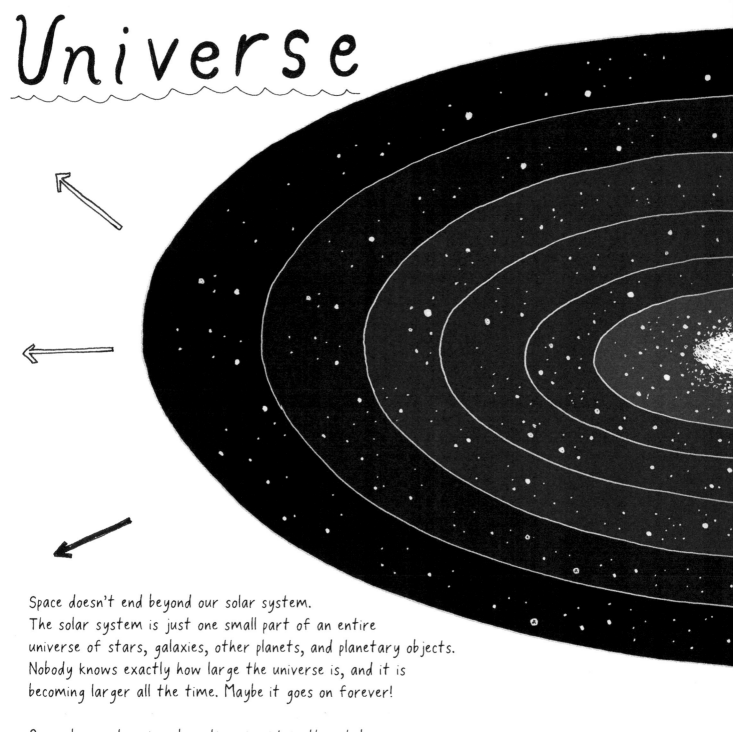

Space doesn't end beyond our solar system.
The solar system is just one small part of an entire
universe of stars, galaxies, other planets, and planetary objects.
Nobody knows exactly how large the universe is, and it is
becoming larger all the time. Maybe it goes on forever!

Our solar system is only a tiny pinprick in the whole universe,
and there are many other solar systems besides our own.

Planet
Marble

Planet
Golf Ball

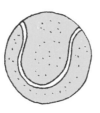

Planet Tennis Ball

Planet Soccer Ball

Planet Basketball

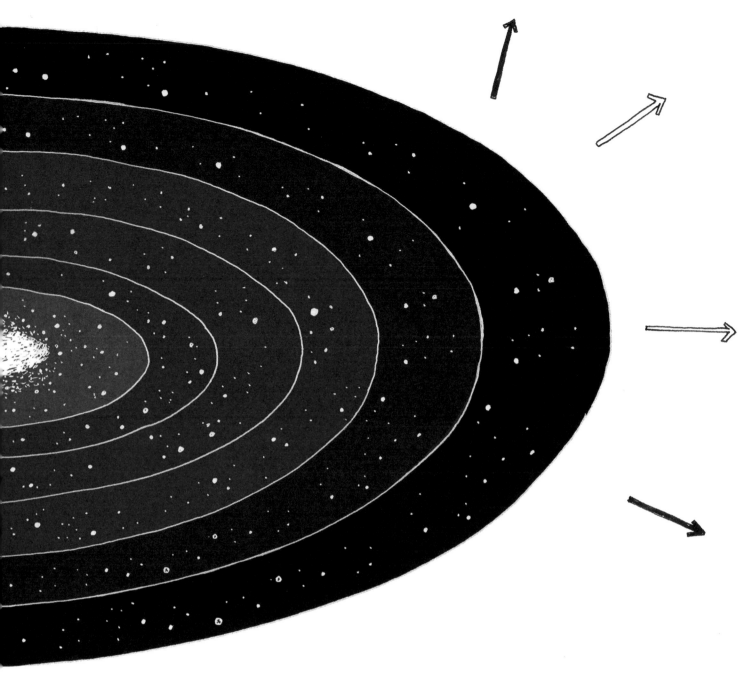

Imagine another solar system. What do the planets look like
and what are their names?

How many are there, and do they have moons? Draw them!

Fruit Solar System

Imagine if the solar system were made of fruit!
Here is how the planets might look.

Make your own!

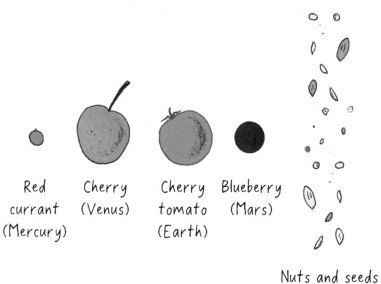

Red
currant
(Mercury)

Cherry
(Venus)

Cherry
tomato
(Earth)

Blueberry
(Mars)

Nuts and seeds
(Asteroid belt)

Watermelon
(Jupiter)

Now cut up your
solar system
to make a planet
fruit salad!

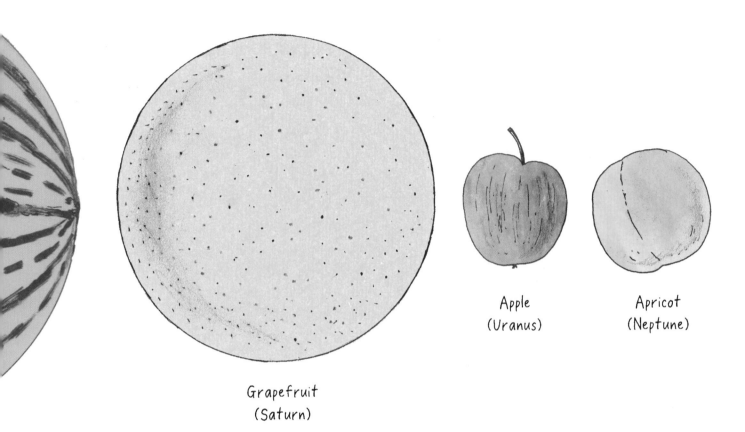

Grapefruit
(Saturn)

Apple
(Uranus)

Apricot
(Neptune)

Draw your fruit salad here.

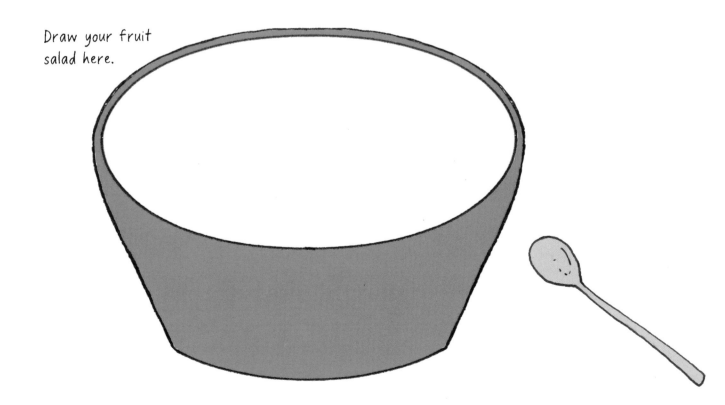

There is no sound in space, because there is no air to carry the sound waves. You can make as much noise as you'd like because no one will be able to hear it!

Draw some more noisy things in space!

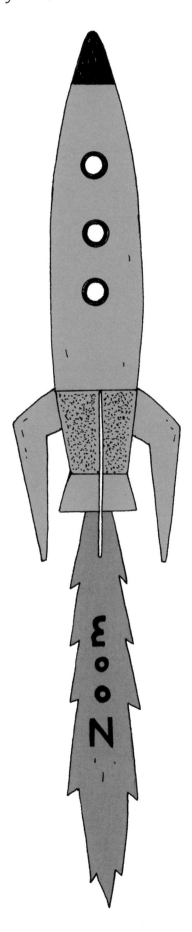

UFOs

There are some strange-looking objects in the sky. They look a bit like UFOs (Unidentified Flying Objects), but are they?

See if you can match the shape to the object.

Can you spot the real UFO?!

Snail

Real UFO?

Cat on a cushion

Hat

Saucepan lid

Cup and saucer

Fried egg

Cake with a
cherry on top

Colander

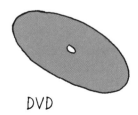

DVD

Space and TIME

How are space and time related?

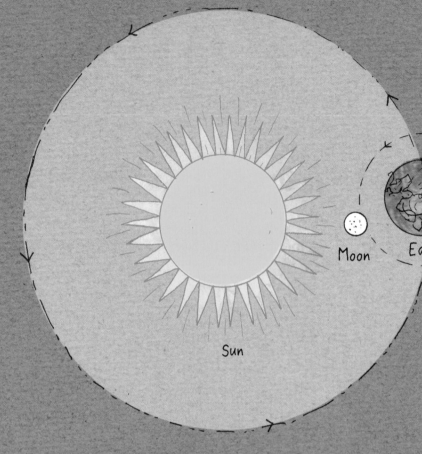

Sun

Moon   Earth

It takes one
year for Earth
to travel around
the sun.

Everything in space is moving all
the time—the Earth is spinning
like a top, although we cannot
feel it. A day is the amount
of time it takes Earth to turn
once on its axis.

A year is the amount of time it takes
for Earth to go around the sun: three
hundred sixty-five and a quarter days.

Years are different lengths on different planets, because each planet takes a different
amount of time to orbit the sun. A year on Mercury is only eighty-eight Earth days,
but a year on Jupiter is equivalent to twelve Earth years!

How old
are you?

Because of this, your age would be very different
if you lived on another planet!

If you have just turned ten Earth years old, your age would be roughly:

41 Mercury years

16 Venus years

10 Earth years

5 Mars years

0.8 Jupiter years

0.1 Uranus years

Imagine if you had a birthday
party on another planet.
What would it look like? Draw it!

Stars

There are many billions of stars in our universe. They are so far away from the Earth that they appear like tiny pinpricks in the night sky.

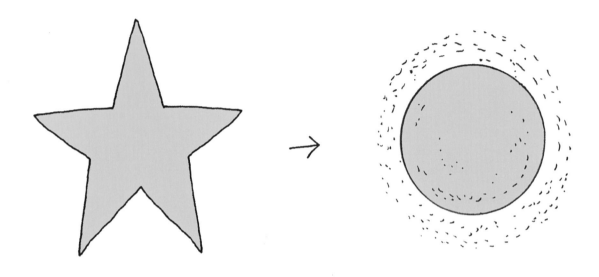

Stars are not star-shaped; they are huge balls of burning gas. The sun is our nearest star.

Although stars appear white, they are actually different colors. The hottest stars are blue and the coolest, red. Color the stars different colors.

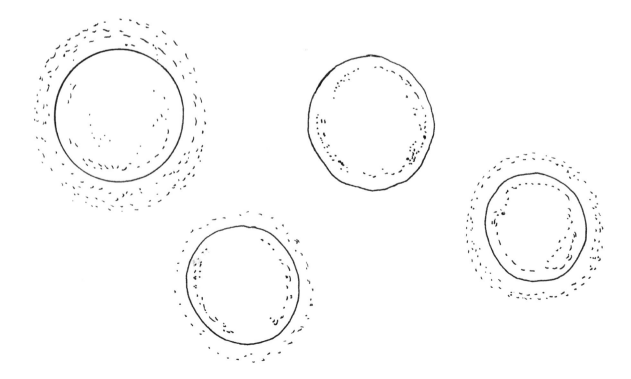

Back in time

Looking at the stars is like looking back in time, because light from the stars takes so long to reach us. Even light from the sun takes eight minutes to reach us.

Distance in space is measured in light-years. A light-year is the distance light can travel in one year, which is actually equivalent to 5,879,000,000,000 miles—a very, very long way!

Light from some faraway stars can take millions, if not billions, of years to reach us here on Earth. This means that we are seeing the star as it was millions or billions of years ago rather than how it is now! Imagine what was happening on Earth 100 million years ago—dinosaurs would have been around! Draw some dinosaurs on Earth.

Ursa Major
(The Great Bear)

Leo (The Lion)

Constellations are
arrangements of stars in the sky.
Some of them are named after animals.

Animals in the Sky

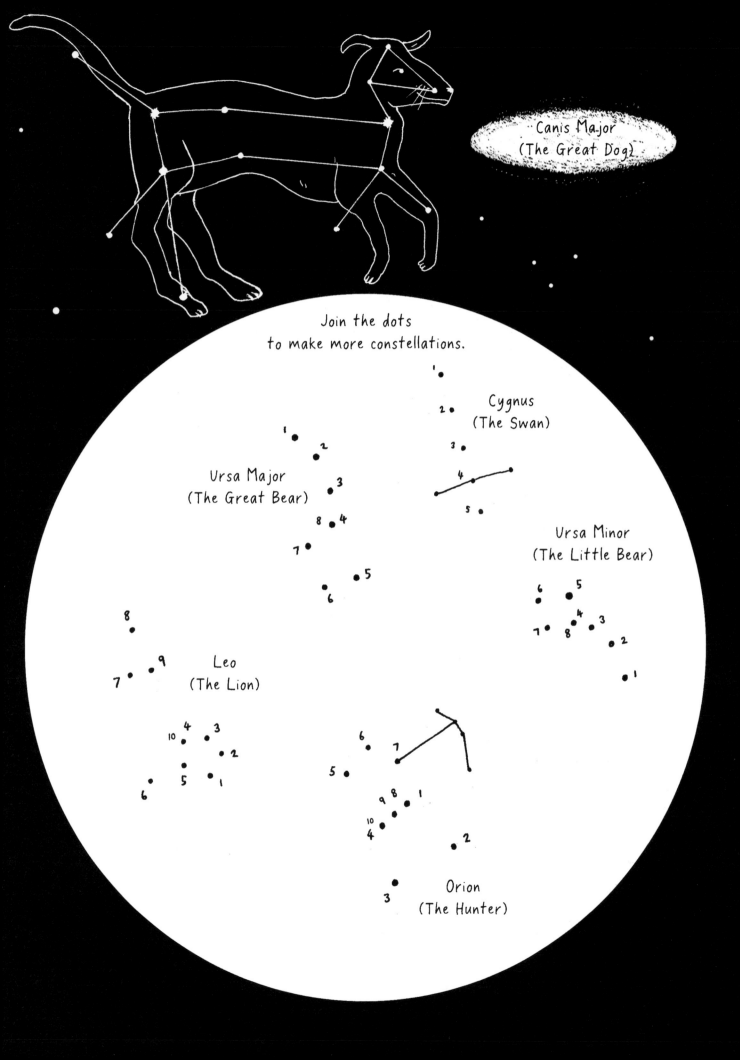

Canis Major
(The Great Dog)

Join the dots
to make more constellations.

Ursa Major
(The Great Bear)

Cygnus
(The Swan)

Ursa Minor
(The Little Bear)

Leo
(The Lion)

Orion
(The Hunter)

The Milky Way

A galaxy contains millions or billions of stars that travel together in space. The name of our home galaxy is the Milky Way. It contains at least 300 billion stars, one of which is our sun.

Galaxies can be different shapes:

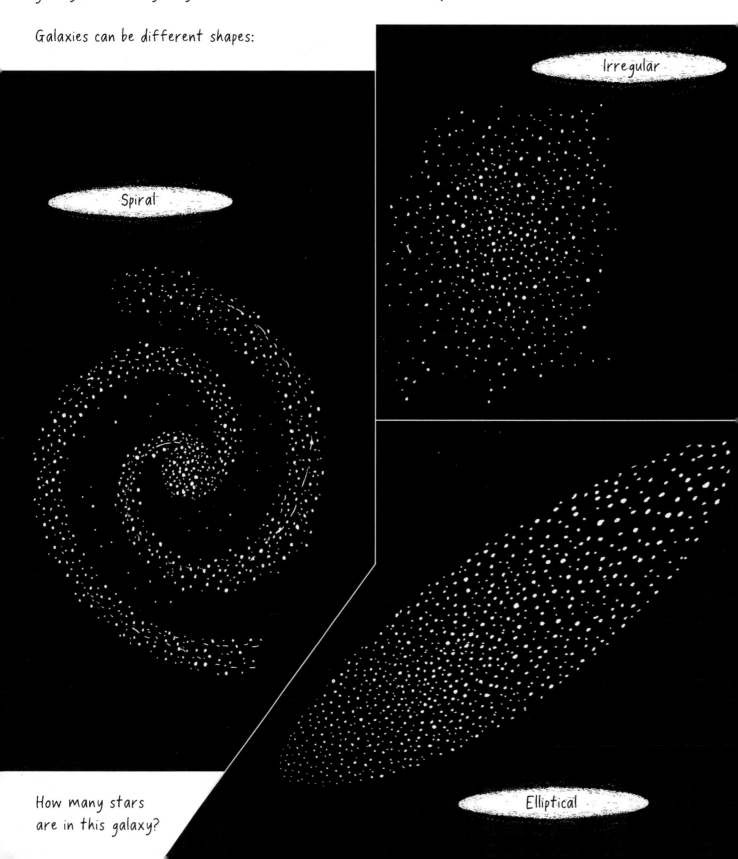

Spiral

Irregular

Elliptical

How many stars are in this galaxy?

Draw your own galaxy!
What kinds of stars are in your galaxy? Here are some other kinds of stars.

Starfish

Star anise

Star fruit

Star jasmine

Star ruby

Star jump

Comets

Comets are some of the most distant objects in orbit around the sun.
They are made of snow, ice, and rocky dust, a bit like a huge, dirty snowball.

They are a rare sight, as they are usually too far away to be seen, but occasionally one comes close to Earth. They appear to have a large, bright tail streaking behind them that is lit up by the sun.

Tail

Head

Sun

The Oort Cloud is made up of billions of comets that stretch all the way around our solar system.
Draw some comets in the Oort Cloud.

Our solar system

Imagine you are having a snowball fight with comets. Draw it!

Where are these aircrafts blasting off to?
Follow the lines to find out!

A cloud

The moon

Venus

Mars

Black Holes

A black hole is a part of space where matter has collapsed in on itself. Black holes suck in everything around them with extremely strong gravity, a bit like a huge, cosmic vacuum cleaner.

Draw some things being sucked in by the vacuum cleaner.

Help!

Astronauts

Astronauts have to wear special suits equipped with oxygen packs that protect them in space and allow them to breathe.

Because there is no gravity in space, astronauts inside a spaceship can float. Draw some astronauts floating inside the spaceship.

Life in Space

Every object on board the spaceship has to be held down, otherwise it would float away!

Astronauts sleep in sleeping bags fitted with straps to hold them down.

Salt and pepper are in liquid form so that the grains don't float away.

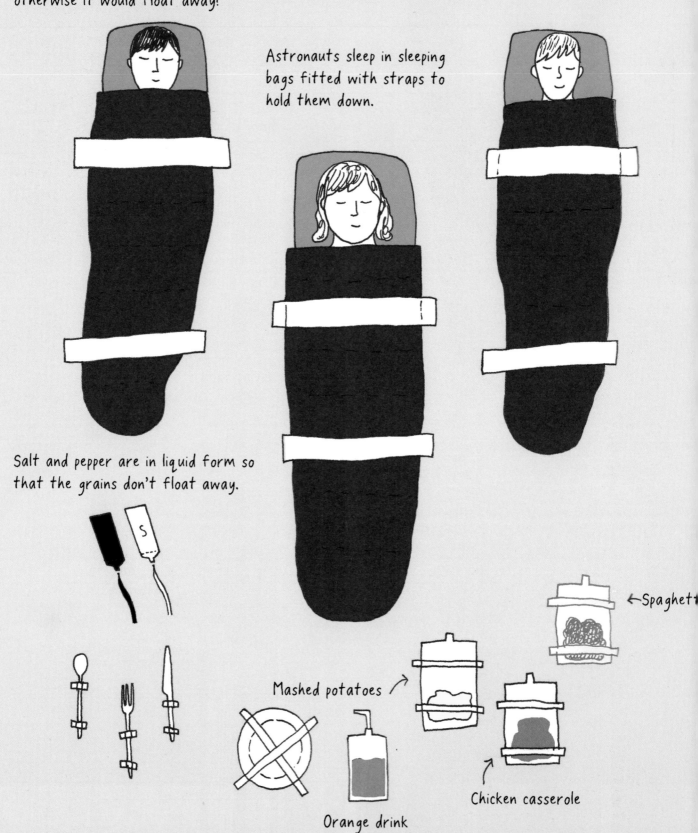

Mashed potatoes

← Spaghetti

Orange drink

Chicken casserole

Cutlery and food also have to be
held down with magnets or Velcro...

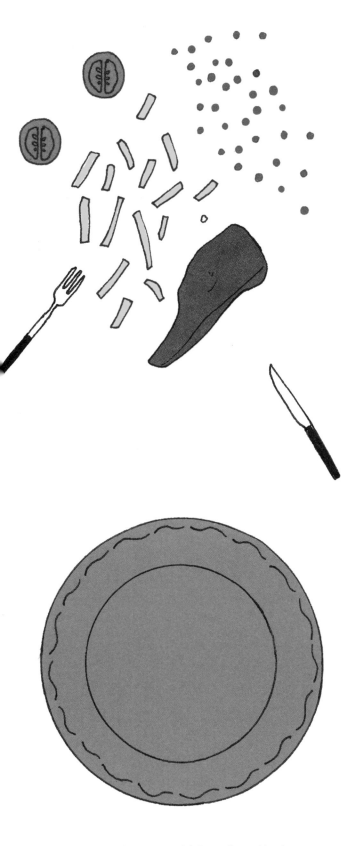

...otherwise they would look like this!

How would your favorite dinner look in space?
Draw it!

In addition to human astronauts, some animals have traveled into space, including dogs, cats, and monkeys.

Help these animals find some treats in space!

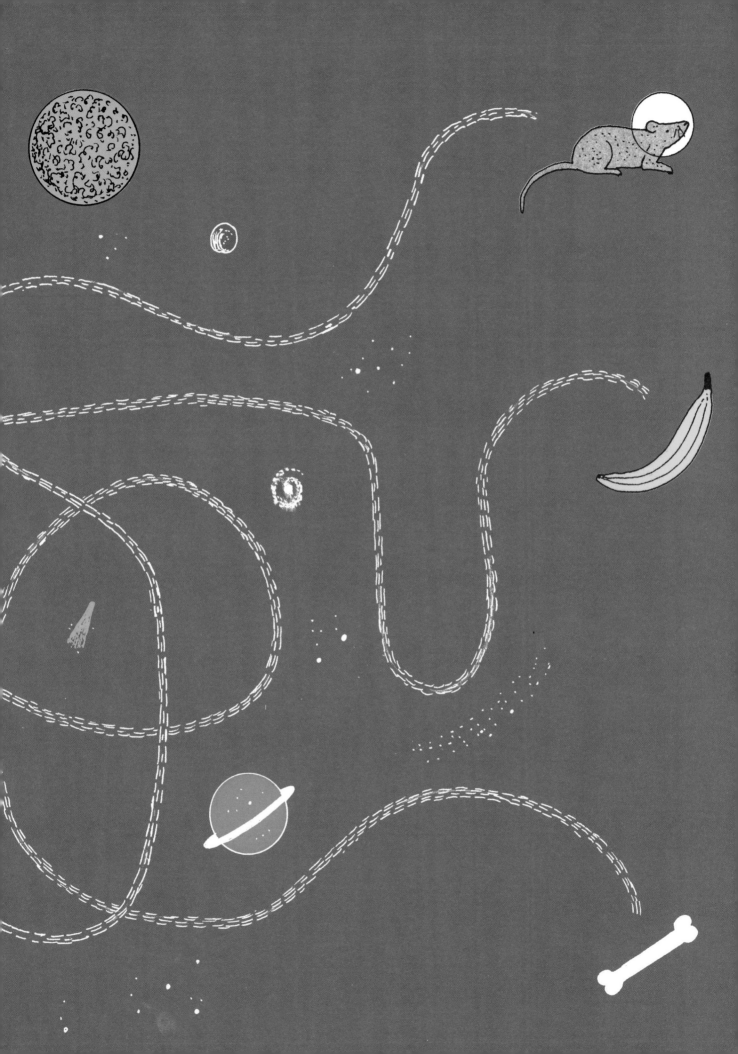

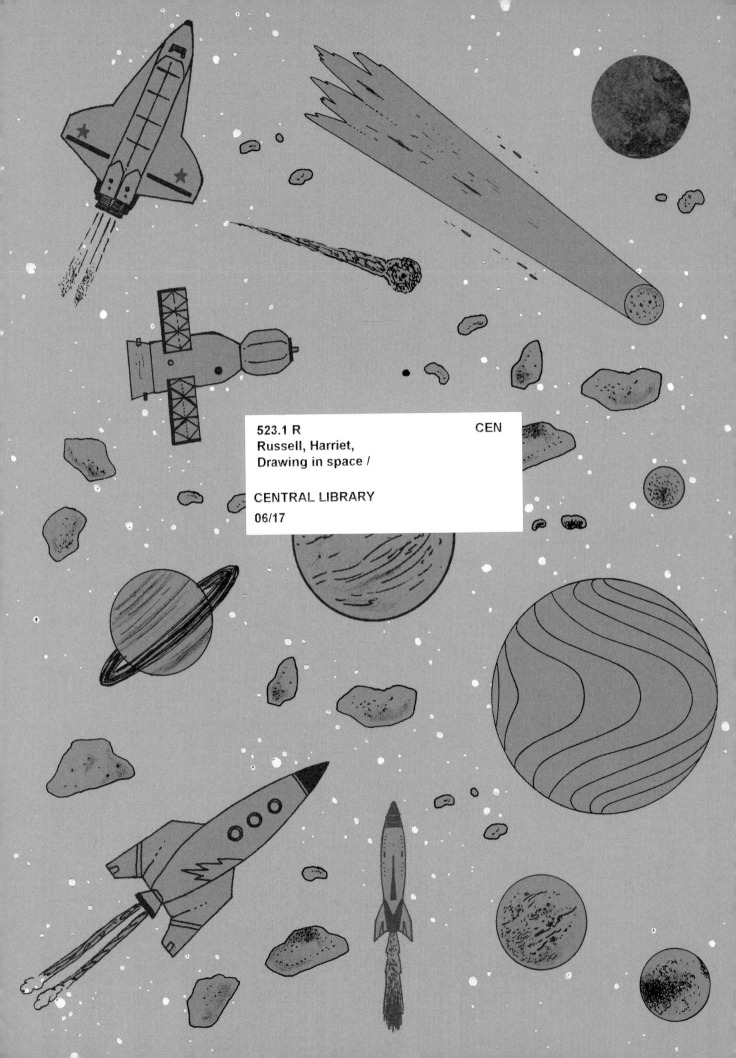

523.1 R   CEN
Russell, Harriet,
Drawing in space /

CENTRAL LIBRARY
06/17